Savannah

To

The Yees

From

Graduation 2014

Date

I am so glad you're a part
of my life. . .

You're sweet!

'Tis you alone that sweetens life. . . .

John Hervey

Love

Kindness in words creates confidence.
Kindness in thinking creates profoundness.
Kindness in giving creates love.

LAO TZU

Love is the true means by which
the world is enjoyed:
our love to others, and others' love to us.

THOMAS TRAHERN

$\mathcal{L}$ove is the master key
that opens the gates of happiness.

OLIVER WENDELL HOLMES

Love is the expansion of two natures
in such fashion that each include the other,
each is enriched by the other.

FELIX ADLER

*The person who tries to live alone
will not succeed as a human being.
His heart withers if it does not
answer another heart.
His mind shrinks away if he hears
only the echoes of his own thoughts
and finds no other inspiration.*

PEARL S. BUCK

*It is only with the heart that
one can see rightly;
what is essential is invisible to the eye.*

ANTOINE DE SAINT-EXUPÉRY

Who could refrain that had
a heart to love and in that heart courage
to make love known?

WILLIAM SHAKESPEARE

The One who died for us—
who was raised to life for us!—is in the presence
of God at this very moment sticking up for us.
Do you think anyone is going to be able to drive a
wedge between us and Christ's love for us?
There is no way! Not trouble, not hard times,
not hatred, not hunger, not homelessness,
not bullying threats, not backstabbing. . .nothing—
nothing living or dead, angelic or demonic,
today or tomorrow, high or low, thinkable
or unthinkable—absolutely nothing can get
between us and God's love because of the way
that Jesus our Master has embraced us.

ROMANS 8:34–39 MSG

*There never was any heart
truly great and generous, that was not also
tender and compassionate.*

ROBERT FROST

*To love deeply in one direction
makes us more loving in all others.*

ANNE-SOPHIE SWETCHINE

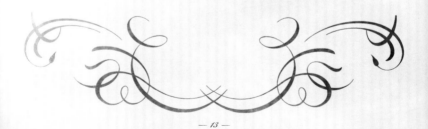

Love is always bestowed as a gift—
freely, willingly, and without expectation. . . .
We don't love to be loved;
we love to love.

LEO BUSCAGLIA

We find rest in those we love,
and we provide a resting place
in ourselves for those who love us.

SAINT BERNARD OF CLAIRVAUX

If I can stop one heart from breaking,

I shall not live in vain.

EMILY DICKINSON

You

Lots of people are poor spellers;

they think the word love is spelled t–i–m–e.

Then, you go ahead and show them

that they're right.

One more reason that I love you!

May no gift be too small to give,

nor too simple to receive,

which is wrapped in thoughtfulness

and tied with love.

L. O. BAIRD

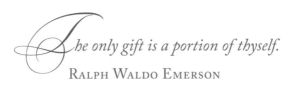

The only gift is a portion of thyself.

RALPH WALDO EMERSON

It is absolutely clear that God has called you to a free life. Just make sure that you don't use this freedom as an excuse to do whatever you want to do and destroy your freedom. Rather, use your freedom to serve one another in love; that's how freedom grows.

GALATIANS 5:13 MSG

*May you enjoy the wide-open spaces
that God provides and run freely
with arms wide open!*

*There is no one like you. . .
your unique set of talents and endless ideas,
so colorful and full of life!*

*God has an intricate plan
to weave your life with
countless others. You are part of a
beautiful masterpiece.*

I know what I'm doing.
I have it all planned out—
plans to take care of you,
not abandon you, plans to give you
the future you hope for.

JEREMIAH 29:11 MSG

You are amazing! God made you in His image.

He created you a little lower than Himself and crowns you with glory!

*Your hands made me and
fashioned me;
Give me understanding
that I may learn.*

PSALM 119:73 NASB

The longer I live,
the more beautiful life becomes.
If you foolishly ignore beauty,
you will soon find yourself
without it. Your life will be
impoverished. But if you invest
in beauty, it will remain
with you all the days of your life.

FRANK LLOYD WRIGHT

Whoever is happy
will make others happy, too.
He who has courage and faith
will never perish in misery.

ANNE FRANK

Happy and blessed are the people
who are in such a case; yes, happy
(blessed, fortunate, prosperous, to be envied)
are the people whose God is the Lord!

PSALM 144:15 AMP

We all die in the end,
but there's no reason
to die in the middle.

PLAYWRIGHT
DAVID MAMET

Grief can take care of itself,
but to get the full value
of a joy you must have somebody
to divide it with.

MARK TWAIN

I love those who can smile in trouble,
who can gather strength from distress,
and grow brave by reflection.
'Tis the business of little minds to shrink,
but they whose heart is firm,
and whose conscience approves their conduct,
will pursue their principles unto death.

Leonardo da Vinci

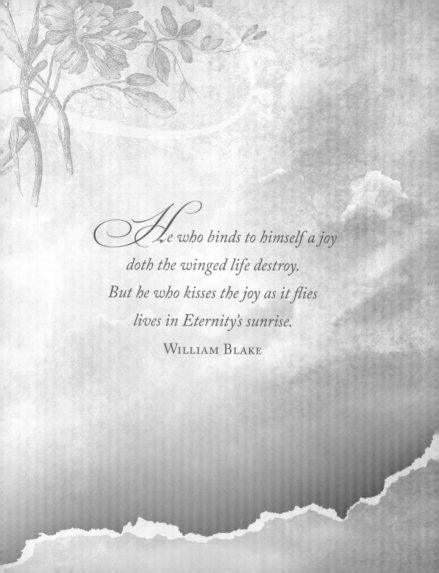

*He who binds to himself a joy
doth the winged life destroy.
But he who kisses the joy as it flies
lives in Eternity's sunrise.*

WILLIAM BLAKE

*God's my island hideaway,
keeps danger far from
the shore, throws garlands
of hosannas around my neck.*

PSALM 32:7 MSG

Joy runs deeper than despair.

CORRIE TEN BOOM

Occasionally in life there are those moments of unutterable fulfillment which cannot be completely explained by those symbols called words. Their meanings can only be articulated by the inaudible language of the heart.

MARTIN LUTHER KING JR.

Joy is a net of love by which you can catch souls. A joyful heart is the inevitable result of a heart burning with love.

MOTHER TERESA

*Real joy comes not from ease or riches
or from the praise of men,
but from doing something worthwhile.*

SIR WILFRED GRENFELL

Joy is not in things, it is in us.

RICHARD WAGNER

Joys divided are increased.

JOSIAH GILBERT HOLLAND

Hope

The LORD directs the steps of the godly.
He delights in every detail of their lives.
Though they stumble, they will never fall,
for the LORD holds them by the hand.

PSALM 37:23–24 NLT

Ah, that is the reason the bird can sing;
on his darkest days he believes in spring.

UNKNOWN

The future belongs to those who believe in the beauty of their dreams.

ELEANOR ROOSEVELT

When the time is right,
up springs new life. No manipulation,
no control; perfect freedom, perfect liberty.

RICHARD FOSTER

It's not what the world brings to you,
it's what you bring to the world.

ANNE OF GREEN GABLES

*Those who bring sunshine to
the lives of others
cannot keep it from themselves.*

UNKNOWN

*The problem with hope
is that you can be disappointed.
But if that hope is rooted in the Eternal God,
there will be no disappointment
upon reaching your destination.*

Nothing is as real as a dream.
The world can change around you,
but your dream will not.
Responsibilities need not erase it.
Duties need not obscure it.
Because the dream is within you,
no one can take it away.

Tom Clancy

When I dream, I am ageless.

ELIZABETH COATSWORTH

Since you are precious in My sight,

Since you are honored and I love you. . .

Do not fear, for I am with you.

ISAIAH 43:4–5 NASB

*It is never too late
to be what you might have been.*

GEORGE ELIOT

Hope is both the earliest and the most indispensable virtue inherent in the state of being alive. If life is to be sustained hope must remain, even where confidence is wounded, trust impaired.

ERIK H. ERIKSON

If you lose hope, somehow you lose
the vitality that keeps life moving,
you lose that courage to be, that quality
that helps you go on in spite of it all.
And so today I still have a dream.

MARTIN LUTHER KING JR.

I am the LORD, your Holy One,
The Creator of Israel, your King.
Thus says the LORD, Who makes a way
through the sea and a path through
the mighty waters. . . . Do not call to mind
the former things, or ponder things of the past.
Behold, I will do something new,
now it will spring forth.

ISAIAH 43:15–16, 18–19 NASB

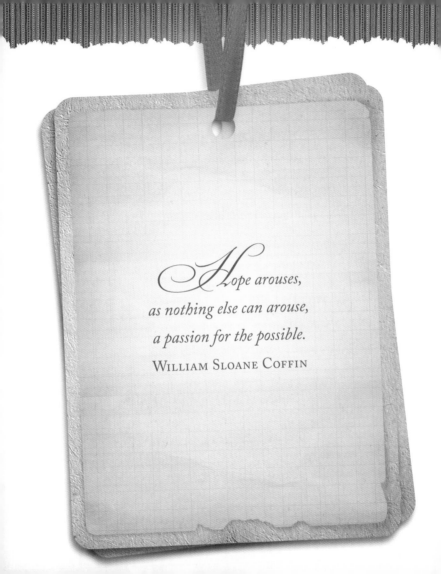

Hope arouses,
as nothing else can arouse,
a passion for the possible.
WILLIAM SLOANE COFFIN

Our Creator would never have made such lovely days, and given us the deep hearts to enjoy them, above and beyond all thought, unless we were meant to be immortal.

NATHANIEL HAWTHORNE

Go confidently in the direction
of your dreams!
Live the life you've imagined.

HENRY DAVID THOREAU

he greatest use of life is to spend it for something that will outlast it.

WILLIAM JAMES

Faith

Faith is the bird that sings when
the dawn is still dark.

RABINDRANATH TAGORE

He who has faith has...
an inward reservoir of courage, hope, confidence,
calmness, and assuring trust that all will
come out well—even though to the world
it may appear to come out most badly.

B. C. FORBES

Faith makes all things possible. . .
love makes all things easy.

UNKNOWN

*A little faith will bring your soul
to heaven, but a lot of faith
will bring heaven to your soul.*

UNKNOWN

I send you tall courage, deep faith,
and unshakable certainty.
Borrow mine if you're temporarily low.

SARK

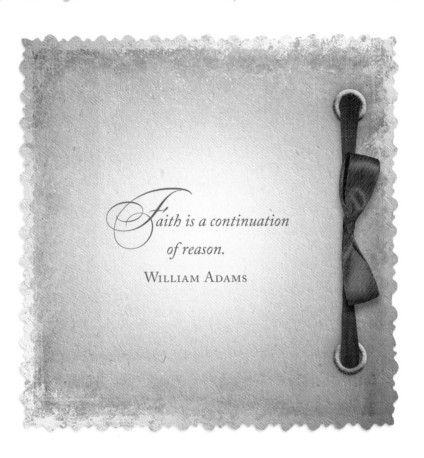

*Faith is a continuation
of reason.*

WILLIAM ADAMS

Where faith is there is courage,
there is fortitude, there is steadfastness
and strength. . . . Faith bestows that sublime
courage that rises superior to the troubles and
disappointments of life, that acknowledges
no defeat except as a step to victory;
that is strong to endure, patient to wait,
and energetic to struggle. . . .
Light up, then, the lamp of faith.

JAMES ALLEN

I look up to the mountains—does my help come from there? My help comes from the LORD, who made heaven and earth! He will not let you stumble; the one who watches over you will not slumber.

PSALM 121:1–3 NLT

The Lord is your keeper;
the Lord is your shade on your right hand.
The sun will not smite you by day,
nor the moon by night.
The Lord will protect you from all evil;
He will keep your soul.
The Lord will guard your going out
and your coming in
From this time forth and forever.

Psalm 121:5–8 nasb